Belly Dancing in a Brown Sweatsuit

Belly Dancing in a Brown Sweatsuit

Poems by

Elaine Sorrentino

© 2025 Elaine Sorrentino. All rights reserved.
This material may not be reproduced in any form, published,
reprinted, recorded, performed, broadcast,
rewritten or redistributed without
the explicit permission of Elaine Sorrentino.
All such actions are strictly prohibited by law.

Cover design by Shay Culligan
Cover image by Paul Hoffman
Author photo by Michelle McGrath

ISBN: 978-1-63980-689-8
Library of Congress Control Number: 2025930528

Kelsay Books
502 South 1040 East, A-119
American Fork, Utah 84003
Kelsaybooks.com

Acknowledgments

Gratitude and appreciation to following publications that curated previous versions of the following poems:

Ekphrastic Review, Niagara Falls Poetry Project: "Spellbound at Niagara"
Etched Onyx Magazine: "Second Thoughts," "Breath Therapy," "On Writing Poetry"
Failed Haiku: "divided nation"
Gyroscope Review: "Finding God in the Tub"
Haikuniverse and *Sappho's Torque:* "bona fide poets"
Haikuniverse: "dilapidated fence," "outdoor bridal shower," "trick or treaters," "foliage," "leaf blowers"
The Keeping Room: "Eye for an Eye"
Lothlorien Poetry Journal: "Before and After," "Irish Twins," "Godmother Sacked," "My Hero"
Muddy River Poetry Review: "Word Association," "The Axe Men Cometh"
ONE ART: "Spelling Things Out"
Panoply: "Don't Let My Wrinkles Fool You"
Poetry Porch: "Sunday Drive"
Quartet Journal: "Belly Dancing in a Brown Sweatsuit"
Sparks of Calliope: "A Moment of Silence for the Salad Bar," "Hands," "Stage Fright"
Spirits Up: "six feel apart"
Verse Virtual: "Planting Season" (formerly "Purpose")
Wilda Morris's Blogspot: "A Magnified Life," "Legacy"
Willawaw Journal: "The Last Gift"
Wingless Dreamer: "Bird Alert"
The Writers' Magazine: "Rappie Cha-Cha"
Writing in a Woman's Voice: "Conflicted," "Lighthouse," "Ambition"
Your Daily Poem: "hoofprints"

Thank you to Sandy D'Entremont and Works in Progress writers for being my first eagle-eye readers, and to editor Eileen Cleary for providing guidance and focus for this collection.

Contents

Before and After	15
Teacups	16
Predator	18
Rappie Cha-Cha	19
Sixteen	21
Conflicted	22
Learning How to Eat Lobster with Grandpa	23
A Magnified Life	24
Haiku Bouquet #1	25
Second Thoughts	26
The Last Gift	28
Bird Alert	30
Missing Out	32
Irish Twins	33
Lessons from Candy Land	34
Spelling Things Out	35
Godmother Sacked	36
Word Association	37
Finding God in the Tub	38
Elephant in the Room	39
Spellbound at Niagara	41
Uninvited	42
Eye for an Eye	43
Breath Therapy	44
Belly Dancing in a Brown Sweatsuit	45
Haiku Bouquet #2	47
Planting Season	48
Hands	49
Stage Fright	50
On Writing Poetry	51
Dear Jesse	52
Ambition	53
Don't Let My Wrinkles Fool You	54

Grocery Shopping with Mom	55
Haiku Bouquet #3	56
The Axe Men Cometh	57
I'm in Love with My Singer	58
A Moment of Silence for the Salad Bar	59
Lighthouse	61
Sharp Edges	62
My Hero	63
Afterlife	64
Sunday Drive	65
Legacy	66

To my husband Ed who encourages creative time,
my sons Daniel and Christopher for their constant inspiration,
and my cousin Sandra whose insight and friendship
helped fashion these pages.

Onward!

Before and After

My life is measured in befores and afters.

Before slimming down
I was a kind, jocular, footloose teen

After, I was self-aware, guarded, judgmental.

Before marrying the wrong man
I romanticized married life

After, I embraced solitude.

Before children
New Year's Eve was about partying

After, New Year's Eve was about staying safe.

Before divorce
the ocean washed my home away

After, home was anywhere my children were.

Before my dad died
life was carefree and celebrated

After, the plane hit the building.

Before my forever man
perfect marriage was a fairytale

After, I was loved unconditionally.

Before cancer
I was undone by mean emails

After, I pressed delete.

Teacups

My six-year-old face appears disfigured
squished against the glass door, anticipating
my uncle's long dark green car

screeching into our driveway,
delivering my daring, dark-haired cousin,
the one who livens up Christmas dinner

with rock-n-roll drumming
while her parents eye roll;
I continue my vigil

tapping on the glass
with my new Penny Brite doll,
decked in her red and white dress,

bow atop her head
prepared for introductions
until my mother spies me,

and in her gentle way
delivers the crushing news,
Sweetie, she's not coming this year

the same heavy sadness
that moved into our house
when Grandma died

amplified after siblings'
disbelief of nothing to divide
but teacups and photographs.

Just make up with him,
my teary scream,
If it were only that easy,
her weighty sigh.

Predator

To the man who exposed himself to us at East Junior High

Warm breezes and green fields
flirted, seducing us to roll
our pudgy, prepubescent bodies
down soft, grassy hills.
We were nine years old.

Our sole concern—
landing in puppy excrement;
down, down, down we tumbled,
until our shadows said *head home*,
and skipping along the cinder track,
we saw a middle school baseball game
in the diamond.

We didn't notice you
in the bleachers,
until you leapt into our path,
Would you like to see me "track" off
is what we thought you said.
We waited for you to run.

Instead, you unzipped,
pulled out your man part
and urinated on the walkway.

Frozen and frightened,
we felt ashamed, wondered
why your stream wasn't yellow,
but milky white.
Then we ran.

Rappie Cha-Cha

Peel, chop, rinse, rinse, rinse,
feed, press, crank, crank, crank;
steps my parents learned not in Arthur Murray's
dance studio, but in their modest childhood kitchens
around the corner from each other in East Boston
where hundreds of French-Canadian families settled
after the Great Acadian Deportation.

Side by side, they peeled twenty
pounds of potatoes, my mother plopping
chunks into the antique hand-cranked grater,
my father forcing the spuds into the cylinder
with a worn wooden block, rhythmically
rotating the cast iron handle,
careful to catch the wet mixture as it oozed
out of the metal contraption
into the waiting bowl.

Shredding complete,
they took an intermission,
long enough for my mother to knead
my father's cramped, numbing digits,
in preparation for the next part,
where she scoops the runny potato mixture
into cheesecloth, and my father uses
his impressive strength to squeeze out
the foamy orange starch.

Their combined performance complete,
now it was time for my mother's solo.

She stirred, stirred, rap-cha-cha
chicken stock into the potato mixture,

buttered the pan, alternated layers of potato
and boiled chicken, rap-cha-cha
topped the pie with generous chunks
of salt pork and placed it in the oven, rap-cha-cha,
first at high heat to crisp the crust, then at lowered heat.

No shortcuts or quick steps
they created in-sync their traditional Acadian dish,
knowing new guests might reject
a giant chicken/potato pancake
with its unusual grey inside and crispy outside,
at first glance more like wallpaper paste.

Mother danced it to the table
smothered in sweet, dark molasses,
unperturbed by a less than stellar review,
knowing someday, like me,
guests may come to love it;
her simple explanation, spoken with a curtsy
Rappie pie is an acquired taste.

Sixteen

The year that started with my head
in the toilet

I stuffed my friends
into the family station wagon
for red light races around the car,

employed small intestines
of a dissected fetal pig
to play jump rope,

voted for class treasurer
based on his athletic build
and tempting, dark eyes.

Unlike today's teens
who endure unspeakable loss,
I was neither civic-minded

nor issue-driven, oblivious
of the turbulence of Watergate,
horrors of Vietnam and Cambodia;

content to shimmy into form-fitting gowns,
curl my long cascade, apply Lip Smackers
and party with friends at Homecoming.

Conflicted

ON MY HONOR
One size-nine foot stuck in childhood,
the other straddles adolescence,
Where do I belong?

I WILL TRY
Right arm, tugged into obedience, shrieks
be courteous, predictable;
rule follower, Girl Scout

TO DO MY DUTY
Left arm, hangs from its socket . . .
what do I do with these new curves,
these feelings, these desires?

TO GOD AND MY COUNTRY
The desire to pursue the genuine me
battles my inclination to obey
shall I survive high school compliant or authentic?

TO HELP OTHER PEOPLE AT ALL TIMES
I want to be sultry, gravelly-voiced Carly,
trading *Kumbaya* for *You're So Vain*;
but in my uniform I forget how to dream.

AND TO OBEY THE GIRL SCOUT LAWS
I unfasten badges and pins from the sash,
tuck them away with the rulebook
and dance with exhilaration down an uncharted path.

Learning How to Eat Lobster with Grandpa

We bonded over dismantling
defenseless boiled shellfish,
sucking Land O' Lakes off our fingertips,

our fifty-three-year gap closed
the moment we fastened on plastic bibs
with giant lobbies on the front

and he launched into crustacean instruction
with his rich French-Canadian accent.
Steakhouse onlookers absorbed

his meticulous tutorial, imitating him
as he twisted off each tiny leg,
bid farewell to the thumb shell,

dipped the delicacy into melted butter
and relished each luxurious bite;
blissful, even as bits of meat flew off

my pick into his lap,
unbridled laughter erupting
from both sides of the table.

A Magnified Life

From behind cupped hands
they whispered *bachelor*
as though he was undesirable,
he hadn't yet met my aunt.

His life, a series of lenses;
black-rimmed kid specs
duck hunter telescope
then high-powered binoculars

to watch birds he appeared to love
more than humans.
He espoused respect
for chickadees, pines, oceans,

the only one to shut off the faucet
when he brushed his teeth in the 60s
explaining to inquisitive nieces and nephews
natural resources are finite;

if he hadn't tumbled from his wheelchair
while birding at eighty-three
I'd thank him for the eye-opening
gift of climate awareness.

Haiku Bouquet #1

dilapidated fence
pig wanders over
for breakfast

outdoor bridal shower
guests unwrap
their umbrellas

divided nation
half want chocolate chip
the other half, sorbet

Second Thoughts

Who can forget
the night you returned
to your dorm
for your warm St. Mark's jacket,

your surprise
at his being there
without your roommate,
his nonchalant shrug

when you tell him
*Marnie's not here
she's out with friends,*
his casual *Yes, I know*.

Who can forget
his predatory advance,
tearing your clothes
throwing you on your bed,

your struggle to deter him
muffling your screams,
the aftermath, your friend's accusations,
his ardent denials

your heartbroken mom
tossing your belongings
into an old suitcase,
removing you from further harm.

Who can forget
the pink indicator,
victim turned mommy
a role you rejected

imagining your relief
when the procedure was over,
the episode behind you,
influencing your Catholic friends

to forever loosen their view,
understanding *choice is a blessing.*
My life is not your life
I still cannot forget.

The Last Gift

Two daughters,
cross-legged
on the hospital floor,
heads down
professors don't wait
until your mother dies.

Neither will they.

Bedclothes barely
rise and fall,
her form
visibly shrunken,
eyelids closed

It's not about me.

Her husband
motions
to the empty
chair,
stay a while

I mention a tape
of peace songs
I've compiled.
My favorite?
I'd Like to Teach the World to Sing.

Then her husband
starts humming
and, from the bed,
her small voice joins in

The girls' heads shoot up
as their mother holds
the whole world in her arms
for the moment, smiles all around.

Bird Alert

Four A.M.
trilling phone
racing feet
Hello?
Uh huh.
Uh huh.
Cerulean warbler!
Where?
Manomet.
Got it.

Rotary dial
makes seven
trips 'round–
waiting,
waiting,
Hello?
It's me.
Cerulean,
Manomet.
Pass it on.

Ornithological
data exchange
complete.

Racing feet,
slamming drawers
dragging tripod
silent house
ticking clock
4:03 A.M. haze
Was I dreaming?

Missing Out

I heard that in the Dagaabe tradition
newborns are entrusted
to the care of grandparents.

I shudder to imagine
what delight I would have forfeited
upon surrendering charge–

no slipping into the nursery
to marvel at slumber
or contemplate fingers, toes

no bundle nesting
in the crook of my elbow,
gazing adoringly at each feeding

no chaotic peace
upon completely abandoning
myself to an innocent

no dopamine-inducing
newborn scent
perfuming my domicile

and no soft cooing
silly hiccups,
or milky smile.

Irish Twins

When folks inquire about my children
I tell them I was twenty-seven when I had my first,
twenty-nine when I had my second.
This is not the whole story.

I fail to share their birthdays are seven weeks apart
or that mine is sandwiched in the middle,
because two years is a more respectable gap
than thirteen months and three weeks.

I omit the part about passion born
out of our Red Sox in the '86 World Series,
the excitement of witnessing victory after victory . . .
interrupted when Buckner and Mother Nature surprised us both.

Lessons from Candy Land

My three-year old sobbed
each time we played Candy Land
and he drew Plumpy the Troll.

The fuzzy oaf sent him tumbling
over the road's blues, reds, oranges, purples
back almost to where he started his climb,

as crushing to him as KEEP OUT
in front of Candy Castle
the moment he thought he'd triumphed.

Are we ever too young to learn
there are things in life
beyond our control?

Spelling Things Out

A tart sip of gimlet soothes her burdened
heart, and loosens her nerve,
she confesses *I cannot believe my son*
does not want his little piece of the sod.

As she positions the tiles for ABSOLVE
on the triple word score, for 45 points,
her surprising instructions open a window,

If you find someone
who makes you happier than my son,
go with him.

Godmother Sacked

Stay away from her,
they instruct you,
as if divorce
were contagious.

Quietly, they remove
you from my influence
assign a new spiritual overseer,
a deferential one who

follows the rules . . .
directives powerful enough
to unravel my purpose
and impact my children's future.

I hope you understand:
sacrificing you
was never my intention.

Word Association

Nothing screams death
more than a plate of bow-tie pasta,
strewn across my mother's faded linoleum,
a marinara runway, from stove to sink.

Honoring his orderly inclinations,
my father's final act—placing his dinner plate
on the table—was interrupted
when his huge heart surrendered,

in less time than butterfly-shaped
farfalle takes to boil.
Before we were prepared to say goodbye,
the ambulance snatched

our fun-loving, ball-tossing,
tire-changing, boo-boo-kissing,
grill-mastering, grandson-adoring,
bug-killing, churchgoing dad,

who sacrificed his carefree retirement
to help his daughter and grandsons.
What will we do without him
we wondered in the hospital

waiting room—blessedly empty
and away from public scrutiny.
Back at my parents' home,
the air empty of his signature whistling,

bow-tie pasta still screamed
from the sauce-laden floor.

Finding God in the Tub

The pink visor and polo uniform
on the cool bathroom floor
reek of burnt coffee
and stale doughnuts.

Warm water soothes my aches
weary fingers work the smooth beads
lips move in silent recitation
Our Father, Hail Mary,

Joyful, Sorrowful, Glorious Mysteries,
searching for relief in prayer,
twenty-seven petition days
twenty-seven more for thanksgiving,

the promise of a way out.
No one witnesses this nightly ritual,
just coffee-pourer and God,
I am confident my answer is on its way.

The response arrives in torrents,
high and low-pressure systems collide,
floods decimate our waterfront neighborhood,
we move to temporary shelter,

I re-evaluate my unorthodox
method of praying in the bath;
could I have elicited this violence of nature?
The takeaway: *Things could be worse.*

Elephant in the Room

Beach ladies arrive at the side door
in nighties and flip flops
late night condolences

offering embraces and stories,
reliving the moment the ambulance
screamed onto the gravel.

Who can sleep with death in the air?

The merry band, now somber,
speak of his tanned, fit physique,
miles trod in worn walking shoes,

his quiet, steadfast resolve,
reliable levelheadedness
when the rest of them partied too long.

What will his wife do without her rock?

Then, *How are you holding up?*
They know daughter-in-law status
is temporary, papers yet to be signed,

neither married nor single,
but grateful for their company
in my eerily silent house,

I search for words to express
the sorrow of losing a father-in-law
and the dilemma that plagues my heart:

How can I console a man
I cannot bear to touch?

Spellbound at Niagara

The last time I knew innocence
I was surrounded by breathtaking

a steady boom over the falls
misting our awe-struck faces

confirmation we are mere specks
in the realm of natural wonders.

I could have lingered there forever
drinking in its mesmerizing thunder

unknowing, balanced on the fraying
thread between well-being and illness

before scalpels, needles, chemical
treatment made their grand entrance;

living in the presence of ferocious power,
I could not get enough.

Uninvited

Cancer comes knocking
once every thirteen years,
and I say *No, thank you,*
but it heaves itself
into my body anyway
refusing to leave
until I escort it to the exit,
thrust it into the dark,
and nail that door shut.

Don't come scratching again.

Eye for an Eye

post-radiation

After I silently counted
the last "six Mississippi"
under the linear accelerator,
lowered my arms
and rolled off the table,
the technician tossed
a fistful of confetti in the air
and handed me a certificate
of completion.

In private that night
after unwrapping
that tender breast
itchy and inflamed,
soothing it with salve,

I folded the beige parchment
once, then once again,
knelt before the fireplace,
threw open the flue,
and struck a match.

Breath Therapy

Sage scorches my nostrils,
I finger the cool wood bordering
my red yoga mat, unable to relax;
what if the house burns down?

Close your eyes,
concentrate on breathing,
free your brain from outside thoughts,
think about how your breath sounds.

I envision life-saving chemo cocktails,
no longer necessary,
exiting my healed body
with every breath,

I don't need you,
I breathe in,
goodbye,
I breathe out.

Belly Dancing in a Brown Sweatsuit

The suit.
Chocolate-colored,
more milk than dark
with a light aqua line racing up the leg,
my little pop of femininity
in otherwise masculine attire
for an activity designed to make one feel
vibrant and sexy
after nine months of treatment.
They said *Wear comfy clothing.*

The instructor.
Dark-haired, exotic, energetic,
smiles as she greets the class
while donning her multicolored hip scarf,
starts shimmying her torso,
her percussive movements rewarded
with a jingling at every thrust,
ends with tiny hip vibrations,
then coaxes her wide-eyed forty-somethings,
Okay ladies, now you try.

We configure ourselves in a line-dancing
pattern and mimic her gyrations,
uncertain how to make our hips snap;
ridiculous and clumsy as she urges,
Let me show you again.

The rebellion.
The women stand, unsmiling, arms crossed

resembling a row of angry Mr. Cleans
but with hair,
they refuse to try it again,
insisting they'd rather watch her dance–
all except for me, the brown-suited belly dancer
who'd already spent too much time on the sidelines.
I'll give it a go.

The solo.
As I shove my stiff arms to the side,
like a department store mannequin,
and move my hips
I hear laughter behind me,
very satisfying, a preferable alternative
to surgery, infusions and radiation,
and I'm happy to provide the amusement
I didn't come to watch.

Haiku Bouquet #2

bona fide poets
spend one short month each year
converting haters

trick-or-treaters asleep
I Google what wine
pairs with Snickers

hoofprints on the roof
I don't believe in Santa
must be unicorns

Planting Season

To avoid dying
my first and second death
simultaneously
I scatter my literary seeds
on fertile ground
in hopes they'll take root.

Hands

in response to the call to arm teachers

My hands, my hands
my blessing hands
caressing hands
finessing hands,
my hands, made for undressing hands;
gentle, unafraid.

My hands, my hands
my kneading hands
my pleading hands
my feeding hands,
my hands, my interceding hands;
passionate and sure.

My hands, my hands
my guiding hands
deciding hands
delighting hands,
my fashioned-for-providing hands;
grateful for their breadth.

My hands, my hands,
my shielding hands
my healing hands
unyielding hands
these peaceful, line-scrawling hands
will never draw a gun.

Stage Fright

I'm a solo act
balancing on the edge
laying bare my courage

eyes shut, I teeter
on the precipice
of dive in or chicken out

when a reassuring hand
touches my elbow,
They're ready for you.

I unclench my eyes
prepared to dip my toe
into unexplored waters

as I step on stage
applause quiets my fears
and I begin.

On Writing Poetry

In the privacy of your own writing
share it with your parakeet
revise, revise, revise

claw your way
to find charm in something
that is not attractive,

less is more,
I disagree,
more is more

I heard it took Robert Frost
only ten minutes to write
Stopping by Woods on a Snowy Evening in 1922,

less than one quarter of an hour;
how long will it take me to perfect
the pull between beauty and obligation?

Dear Jesse

Dearest Cousin Jesse
I've been meaning to ask you
why you prefer this abbreviated
version of your name.

My name is plain, Elaine, Elaine
but yours has that lovely
little feminine flourish at the end
Jessica, ica, ica . . .

How I've longed for more
than that silent final vowel,
envious of every Leilani,
Indigo, Alessandra

Elaine, functional enough
is like a broken-in pair
of cowboy boots
a name unnoticed until Jerry

Seinfeld's ex-girlfriend
made the name fashionable
for someone considered
one of the guys.

Ambition

Where are you ambition
I cannot find you anywhere
you refuse to be coaxed
from in front of the screen,
nor finessed
into abandoning your sweats.

You are neither at the bottom
of a wine glass
nor hidden in a bag of Ruffles,
I cannot sauté you into being
when you are not in the pan.

Another installment
of *Gilmore Girls*
or a round of *Words with Friends*
has yet to ignite
the extinguished flame.

I flounder
close to shore
hoping someone will lay out a feast
of inspiration
so I might celebrate
even a fleeting sense of accomplishment.

Don't Let My Wrinkles Fool You

This is not the final version of me:

there's the one where five A.M. is the perfect time
to play peek-a-boo with a grandchild;

the one where I am no longer considered a cog,
but the mastermind;

the one where my journey to Italy
yields fresh olives and newly-pressed oil;

the one where I don't keep time
to someone else's clock;

the one where purple and green ink
autograph my first book;

the one where I drink in the view from the Rocky Mountaineer
as it winds its way from Vancouver to Banff;

the one where I sneak chocolate
to the naughty child in the corner;

the one where I compose
my own ending.

Grocery Shopping with Mom

At eighty-four,
she delights at the candy aisle,
eyes aglow
at the colorful cellophane packages.

This is what my cleaning lady likes best.

Thoughtful in the choosing,
she carefully plucks one
package of hard candy
and one package of soft,
depending upon who
might visit that week,
and drops them into her cart
with other items she'll donate
to the food pantry.

Haiku Bouquet #3

six feet apart
no one told the birds
at the feeder

foliage
nature's attempt at beauty
before death

leaf blowers roar
my husband
lovingly combs the lawn

The Axe Men Cometh

Avon shades—ripe cherry,
champagne frost, coral flame
create a patchwork smudge

in the emptied makeup drawer
of my mother's '50s-style triple dresser,
awaiting its fate on her three-season porch.

No relatives high-hosey'd them
no looky-loos to appreciate
bedroom furnishings, dry sink, roll-top,

days from the property closing,
hard decisions necessary,
we placed the call

and should have known,
seeing JUNK splayed across
the side of their box truck;

but the men gingerly remove
each treasure, careful not to ding
the wood around her door,

an altered approach at the curb
splintering each piece with an axe
for more suitable transport.

Watching my childhood furniture
smashed is jarring as watching
birds fly into windmills.

I beg them to stop
but they are on a tight schedule.

I'm in Love with My Singer

We forged a friendship
when the kids were small, money tight,
the unexpected birthday gift
that screamed of possibility;

this machine with its basic
straight and basting stitches,
its practical and fun zigzag,
and other sexier designs

I later learned had names
like Scallop, Icicle and Diamond,
all contributing to the creation
of shiny silver knight costumes,

long-tailed green dragons
with gold bellies and oversized paws,
quilted Christmas stockings
with each child's name on the cuff,

customized curtains, seat cushions,
wall hangings, baby jumpers
placemats and card holders,
who can forget wide wale corduroy

knickers for the high school
version of *Carousel,*
all tailored with my reliable
indestructible sewing machine.

Like many partnerships
ours did not endure quarantine,
it planted its mask-making foot
by jamming in reverse.

A Moment of Silence for the Salad Bar

Curtains to the possibility
of sesame cabbage salad
and tapioca pudding
building a relationship
in the same takeout container,

Adios to sidling up to the bar,
surreptitiously
elbowing my way
to the last pickled beet
among the vinegary cornucopia;

the heavy-weight champion
of abundant choices
as appealing as hitching a ride,
putting Noxema on a sunburn,
or helmet-free biking,

even the sexy plexi
has repurposed itself since 2020,
now guarding teenage cashiers,
instead of red bell peppers,
from sneezers and viruses.

I miss sneaky side glances,
pretending I'm not eyeing
the tempting veggie-protein combo
composed by the stranger beside me
with a chill-seeking palate;

Goodbye to eight different lettuces,
the thrill of topping tuna salad
with pickles and sunflower seeds,
and daring to pluck tomatoes
and red onion with the same tongs.

Lighthouse

On the other side
of the bathroom door
my mother whimpers

God, help me
I don't know what to do
I don't know what to do,

forgetting I exist
the moment
the latch catches.

I touch the wood
wondering
am I her lighthouse
or am I underwater myself?

Sharp Edges

My frame has no more sharp edges.
smooth as sea glass buried under sand and shell.

Vanished is the shelf that rocked back and forth,
repetitive and soothing for my children,

In my sleep I still reach for the sharpness,
startling myself awake when I cannot find it,

like an amputee searching a long-released limb
feeling instead, insatiable longing.

My Hero

She tattooed swooping sideburns
and intricate Irish symbols
in vibrant blues and greens
on her exposed scalp
when alopecia knocked.

I couldn't unhitch the parachute, freefall
I'd choose the wig,
perhaps hair replacement,
but never sterilized needles
with their mandatory repeat performance
every few years.

She never judged,
this maverick
who cuts my aging, thinning locks,
she calls her radiant self a freak.

Afterlife

They say I'll boast
a full head of hair,
my once long, dark
cascade, pulled back,
swept up, braided
like a fishtail,
wrapped at my crown,
or hanging loose
for my lover
to savor in his kiss.

Sunday Drive

Along the Belfast to Augusta highway
tires hum in steady rhythm.

It was the farthest north they had ever been,
green fields left

green fields right.
Easy laughter jolts them back

to the family reunion
now in the rear-view mirror.

Ten winged bodies rise up
from the driver's side.

Unable to maneuver.
Impact unavoidable.

Matted feathers and blood mar
the mangled grating of the blue Sienna.

Inside, heartbreak weighs heavy,
Outside, eight turkeys touch down.

Legacy

After condolences
have been accepted
and teary-eyed guests devour
the last éclair,
my two boys will close the door,
loosen their ties,
kick up their feet,
and pick up my orphaned computer
to discover my secrets
in verse.

They'll discover
I sometimes colored outside the lines.

About the Author

Poet Elaine Sorrentino is Communications Director at South Shore Conservatory in Hingham, MA, where she creates promotional and first-person content for press and for a blog called SSC Musings.

Her poetry has been published online and in print in blogs and journals such as *Minerva Rising, Willawaw Journal, Glass: A Journal of Poetry, Gyroscope Review, Ekphrastic Review, Quartet Journal, Writing in a Woman's Voice, ONE ART: a journal of poetry, Muddy River Poetry Review, Etched Onyx Magazine,* and *Haikuniverse.* She is facilitator of the Duxbury Poetry Circle.

A two-time breast cancer survivor, Elaine, along with poet Dzvinia Orlowsky, founded a program called Pink LemonAid, where writers, artists, and musicians are invited to share art inspired by their experience with breast cancer—either as a survivor or as support for a loved one.

Elaine lives in Pembroke, Massachusetts with her musician husband and various farm animals who wander into their yard.

www.ingramcontent.com/pod-product-compliance
Lightning Source LLC
Chambersburg PA
CBHW030914170426
43193CB00009BA/843